NO DAY AT THE BEACH

Wisconsin Poetry Series

Edited by Ronald Wallace and Sean Bishop

NO DAY AT THE BEACH

JOHN BREHM

The University of Wisconsin Press

Publication of this book has been made possible, in part, through support from the Brittingham Trust.

The University of Wisconsin Press
728 State Street, Suite 443
Madison, Wisconsin 53706
uwpress.wisc.edu

Gray's Inn House, 127 Clerkenwell Road
London EC1R 5DB, United Kingdom
eurospanbookstore.com

Printed in the United States of America
This book may be available in a digital edition.

Library of Congress Cataloging-in-Publication Data
Names: Brehm, John, 1955– author.
Title: No day at the beach / John Brehm.
Other titles: Wisconsin poetry series.
Description: Madison, Wisconsin : The University of Wisconsin Press,
            [2020] | Series: Wisconsin poetry series
Identifiers: LCCN 2019039025 | ISBN 9780299326548 (paperback)
Subjects: LCGFT: Poetry.
Classification: LCC PS3602.R444 N6 2020 | DDC 811/.6—dc23
LC record available at https://lccn.loc.gov/2019039025

For Alice

CONTENTS

⏽

⏽⏽

Back Then

Everything was better back then.
Even my nostalgia was better,
more piercing, more true.
I miss missing things that much,
but not as much as I missed
missing things back then.
Even my anxieties about the future,
which have indeed come to pass,
were more vivid back then,
more real. Reality itself seemed
more real back then—this clanking
stage play only a fool could find
convincing—I fell for it all,
and it killed me, again and again.
Ghosts of myself wander
the cities I've lived in, thinking
of other cities, imagining me
here imagining them.
We nod to each other across
the years, the way the last line
of a poem will sometimes
look back, wistfully,
at the first.

Tough Town

Squirrels
knocked

it down
three

days
ago but

a puffed-
up finch

keeps
staring at

where
the bird-

feeder
used to be.

Swifts

for my father

Early fall, the light thin and brittle, and if
it's true that deprivation is a gift,
I accept the gift. I walk down
to Wallace Park to watch the swifts
that roost every September
in the Chapman School's tall
brick chimney. The charming swifts
with their long, forked tails
and swept-back wings,
ten thousand of them swerving
and darting in the evening sky,
a flowing, expandable spiral
of birds, clearing the air of insects
and riveting the wandering
human mind. Tonight there must be
three hundred spectators,
a whole hillside of us, ordinary people
whose wings fell off eons ago,
who traded flight for speech
and have regretted it ever since,
sodden and earthbound as we are,
except for our lifted eyes, our *oohs* and *ahs*
that show we're still alive when
the peregrine falcon dives in
and knifes one out of the air,
which we boo or cheer,
sometimes simultaneously.
We love this passion play of form
and formlessness,

the birds' shifting patterns
flung out like a whiplash of water
or school of fish above
the stationary human school,
then drawn tight together,
a miracle they don't crash into each other,
a miracle of echolocation, until
you see them as they truly are:
a single organism, a body made mostly
of air and quick decisions, jagged
motions that gradually cohere—
a poem, in other words.
It takes the flock a full twenty minutes
to funnel down into the chimney,
and it seems a living smoke
pulled back into a still and sleeping fire,
so beautiful I forget for a moment
my father's death, or I turn my mind
away from it or, no, I open
my grief to accommodate this wonder
and wonder what he might have thought of it,
were we standing here together,
the kind of thing we never did, and now
will never do, except in my imagination—
that unchanging inner sky where the swifts
take flight whenever I want them to
and my father cannot die.

Wishful Thinking

The train drags its urgent
mournful flaglike
sound all the way
from the nineteenth century—
why not? the past
isn't really gone
and rain falls and
falls and never gets up
it lies in flat black
pools on the tar-
paper rooftop
of the two-car
garage across the
alley under a gray
invariable sky—
rains like this
must have driven
the cave painters
into caves where they
ate mushrooms
and tripped on
down to utter
darkness to work
by torchlight
with crushed rock
and some say animal
blood but I don't
think so—
I wish they'd

show up here and
paint this day
(it's just like a cave)
a different color
people it with beasts
and half-human
half-animal beings
I wish I were one
of those I mean truly
not just the way
I already am.

Sleeping in the Wind

it is a mistake
being incarnate
—Lucia Perillo

How beautiful it will be to be
a wind without a body,
a swift unfolding curvature
of air, slightly lighter,
or heavier, than standing air,

flickering a candleflame in Tibet
or tousling the hair
of a woman falling in love;
carrying off the stench
of a massacre, dissolving it,

then coming back cleanly to be
breathed by murderers and
mourners alike. Is that
what it will be like—
after this creaking sideshow

we watch from the cheap seats
of ourselves, the hands
crippling up, in constant pain,
the back proving the foolishness
of walking upright again

and again, the trees still calling us
to live up there, safely out
of sight, at ease above the earth,
harmless and free from these
imperfect accommodations,

caressed by and sleeping in
the wind we will become?

The Dismal Kingdom

Sky so low and dark and gray
it might as well be
a stationary
ocean overhead.
The Black Sea perhaps.
We look up and swear
the birds have turned to fish,
swimming listlessly
in monotone
cloud-shallows.
Dream-smothering skies,
the imagination
held down,
refracted back to us,
emptied of all
but the smallest
waterlogged ambitions.
A paradise for trees,
of course,
their leafy dispositions
rooted equally in
earth and air,
as ours are.
But they lord it over us—
their magnificent nonchalance
cuts us down to size.
It rains so long
and unrelentingly
things lose their shadows,
or are absorbed by them;
daylight becomes

a secondhand, pawnshop
kind of darkness,
and even our thoughts
turn mossy.
All winter long
we walk with our
heads down, minds flat
against the hard gray ground.

Cold Spell

Fourth day
of snow

freezing rain
huge

avalanches
of wind—

yesterday
a dozen

crows
lined the

telephone
wires

puffed up
and

pissed off
jutting

their heads
forward

to shriek
at the world

as well
they should.

Wisteria

I rarely get ideas and when
I do they're too small
to be largely untrue
like loneliness is
inescapable
is it really? yes
I think so
but tomorrow
I could change
my mind if not
my condition—
a month ago
wisteria emerged
from the invisible
world like dense
clouds of grapes
and hung in
dreamy splendor
for a few weeks
and now of course
they're gone—
everything
happens like that
people plants
animals appearing
like a magic trick
and then vanishing
back into what
the old Taoists

called the un-
manifested
everything except
loneliness
which does not exist
but is everlasting
nevertheless.

The Vow

Because you were coming over
I cleaned my apartment,
threw away stacks of paper
without looking at them—
poems and bills (they'll send
them again), flyers
for events I would not attend,
magazines I had not read,
nor even opened, coupons
I would never redeem,
forms I should have filled out
long ago, a parking ticket?
I hoisted a box of books
that had sat on the floor
for six months to the top shelf
of the hall closet. Made my bed,
neatly. Even got new dishes,
of an intricate Turkish
design, and washed them
before stacking them
in the cupboard, something
I'd never done before (how dirty
can they be—they're *new*,
for God's sake!).
I swept the floors, dusted
every surface, even moved a chair
to abolish the little tumbleweeds
of lint and fallen hair,
sloughed-off skin
and felt-like entanglements
gathering underneath.

I scrubbed the tub and took
a long abrasive bath.
I was a clean person
in a clean space cleanly waiting.
What could be more perfect?
But you did not come over.
So I sat in my suddenly tidy
apartment, held my head
in my hands and felt ridiculous.
At least my place is clean,
I thought: open, spacious, spare.
And I made a vow to keep it
that way, knowing full well
I would break it.

Loss and Gain

The rich black
soil of

failure
is where

I plant
my seeds

their
fruition

is no
fruition—

cool shade
of non-

existent
trees.

Dharma Talk

He said changing nothing changes
everything, which if you change

the words around also suggests
that changing everything

changes nothing,
which further implies

that nothing and everything
are interchangeable, are

in fact the same thing, or
the same non-thing, having

no fixed, unchanging nature,
or a nature that is in constant

change, if change can be said
to be constant, and is therefore

a kind of emptiness about
which it is better to speak

only in the negative, of
what it is not, or not

to speak at all.

Fedora

I have a sweaty, hat-ruining head.
My straw fedora sports a ring
of darkish discoloration
around the brim.
Luckily I'm tall, so only God
can see it and it hardly
bothers Him,
though it worries me.
It's on my list of things
to worry about: money,
relationships, my career, ha!,
the jittery hummingbird
of my heart, the shocking
scarcity of jazz clubs
here in Portland, Oregon
(why, oh why, did I leave
New York?), my father's dying,
my mother's loneliness.
Sweat stains on my hat
sometimes rise
to the top of the list.
Which shows what kind
of person I am, frivolous
and vain, though I like
to think myself otherwise.
I wear the fedora even
when hiking in the heat
of summer, knowing it will make
the sweat stains worse.
Why? Because a beautiful woman
once smiled at me on the trail,

and I'm sure it was partly
due to my hat, so stylish
and unexpectedly debonair
in the bright green forest.
She was not tall. She could not
see what my worrisome
head had done to it.

Delayed Response

I used to turn
some

heads
but now

I am
invisible—

a super-
power

wished
for as

a child
and

granted
by an

all-seeing
God at last.

Looking on the Bright Side

Death: at least it'll give me a chance to catch up
on my sleep. No more tossing and turning
worrying about what's going to happen next.
Unless of course my dreams of dancing girls
and hookah parties come true.
In which case it'll give me a chance
to catch up on all the fun I missed
being too tired from lack of sleep.
A win-win situation.
Unless of course the dancing girls turn out to be
my former lovers, flitting before me
with vengeful or disdainful expressions
on their still painfully lovely faces.
In which case I can go on writing the poems
of failed love that failed to make me
famous when I was alive.
A suitable way to while away eternity.
Unless of course the hookahs are filled
not with tobacco but with heavenly peyote
(food of the gods the gods left for us),
in which case it'll give me a chance
to catch up on the deathless bliss
of boundless mystical oneness
my fear of death always kept me
from fully experiencing
here and now.

Right Speech

It used to be I would say anything
to be funny, even if it hurt
other people's feelings.
One night at a steakhouse
in Phoenix when my nephew
sent his steak back because it was
too rare, the waitress asked:
"So, we should cook it more?"
And I said, "No, cook it *less.*"
Which was funny, but not to her,
and she probably spat on the meat
or dropped it on the floor,
thereby punishing my nephew
but not me who deserved it.
A friend of mine who worked
at a diner years ago said:
"Don't send your food back."
"Why not?" I said. "Trust me,"
he said, "don't send your food back."
You could see the terrible things
cooks do to food sent back
forming in his mind's eye and on his face
a grim amusement with undertones
of vengefulness. But I hadn't yet
met him when I made the smart remark
to the waitress and my nephew hadn't
yet died. His death was still
a long way off, it was still lacing up
its boots, studying the maps,
while we went on talking
as if we'd live forever.

Falling Hours

No one can tell how
the metaphors we live by
may be fulfilled.
Five years ago I lay
with my belly
cut open, in Kyoto,
surrounded by surgeons—
nine hours
plunged into
memoryless darkness,
my nephew
lying next to me.
They lifted half
my tender, viscous liver,
held it like a fish pulled from
the ocean depths
of the body,
and gave it to him,
a gift he did not refuse
but which could
not save him.
I remember
the sleepless night before,
walking down
to the 24-hour
convenience store
in the hospital basement
to buy a clock so I could watch
the hours fall away,
the last hours
of my life as someone

who had merely *felt*
cut open.
The hallways empty,
3 a.m. fluorescent lights
in the transplant ward
giving off
a frazzled hum
of desolation,
the nurse
at the nurses' station,
her eyebrows popping up
like question marks
when she saw me
pass by.
I still have the clock,
silver and black and cheaply made
(plastic, not brass or steel)
but trustworthy nonetheless.
It has a button
on the side you can press
to light up its face
so you can see
the time
in the darkness.
That clock was there—
it held those hours
in its dominion,
its hands
swept through them.
I keep it on my nightstand
like something
brought back from a dream
to prove
that it was real.

November

Look at them
they've

fallen and
still

they fling
themselves

shamelessly
joyously

across the
grass—don't

they know
they're

no longer
alive?

Signs and Wonderings

When I see the inevitable bad puns of hair salons
—*Hair Apparent, A Cut Above, Hair Force,*
Julius Scissor, Hair We Are, etc.—I think
how painful it must be to answer the phone:
"*Curl Up and Dye,* how can I help you?"
Well, you can start by changing the name
of your salon to something simple like *Shirley's*
Style and Cut, or *Pam's Perms,* or *Main Street*
Hair Salon, and leave the puns to professionals
like myself who once impressed everyone
at a rooftop party in Brooklyn when a colleague
asked "Do the French roll their *r's*?" and I said
"They roll their *eyes.*" Or when at the Indian
restaurant, I said "We could start with some *naan,*
but that would be a *naan starter,*" which has
the virtue of being both a pun and paradox.
A professor of mine in grad school once said:
"A pun is two words competing for the same
semantic space." Yes, but why must everything
be a competition? Or a question of space,
of trying to occupy or empty it? "What kind of pie
are you having today, sir?" "I'm having the Occu-pie."
"How is it?" "It's terrible, but it fills me up."
And is that what we all want, to be filled up,
with food or words or love or hatred or memories?
With ideas, beliefs, opinions? Of what use are they?
I used to think I wanted to be empty, but once
on magic mushrooms I felt my mind was being
sucked out of my head, pulled into the void,
and it terrified me. I very much wanted that
not to happen. "Ego death," I later later learned

was how Terence McKenna describes the experience,
which makes me wish I'd surrendered to it, gone
through that portal into shimmering dissolution,
to reemerge—as what? More open, more awestruck,
less tightly clenched around my fears and desires?
Now I imagine actual death, or try to.
The mind can't really conceive its nonexistence,
can't create a space where it enacts its own undoing.
But to think of death, to write about it, is that
a way to call it forth? Does death listen to us,
cock its ear like a dog when it hears us
speak its name? I wondered about that last night,
after reading about the brilliant young neurosurgeon
who gets lung cancer and knows he's going to die
and has to tell himself all the things he told
his patients. I tell myself—I tell others, too—
that I'm not afraid of death, but last night it felt
more real, that it's going to happen, that I won't
be *me* anymore, won't be here, or anywhere.
It was as if death had heard me and said "Oh, really?
Not afraid? Are you *sure*?" Here in Oregon
trees compete for the same space and life
and death are intertwined, rooted together,
entangled in earth and air, as a seed will fall
on a fallen tree, a Douglas fir or cedar
or redwood, some mossy beast lying prone
beside a ravine, and begin to rise up, drawing on
the nutrients of the trunk decomposing beneath it,
an opportunist we might say, lifting itself into the sky.
And sometimes when the dead tree is wholly gone,
has become air, the space it occupied will remain,
an opening, a reminder of where death became life,
and the new tree's roots reach down, drip down,

around that emptiness to hold itself upright for,
if it's lucky, a few hundred years. I leave it to you
to grasp the implications, the possibilities for
metaphor, in this unfolding forest parable. But now,
as the year is ending, I wonder if time itself works
that way—one day, or week, or year, or moment,
growing out of the death of the previous one,
or if the dissolution of individual consciousness
at death nourishes a larger consciousness,
or if the spirit, the breath-spirit, is released at last
to fly around and observe with infinite
compassion the infinite folly of the living,
perhaps now and then to intervene.
Impossible questions! But maybe I'll
call the *Curl Up and Dye* hair salon
and ask them just the same.

Blathery Performance

Sometimes the ego is a one-man marching band,
high-stepping down main street, pounding a bass drum
with one hand, mouth-farting through a tuba with the other.
That's how I feel, anyway, when I look back at some
of my blathery performances, where I sharpen my wit
on other people's weaknesses, reel off judgments
and opinions like decrees, jump on every opportunity
to say something funny, however hurtful it might be.
When I asked a friend to give me the gossip
about a certain writers workshop
where I teach once a year, she said there's
tension around who has to drive visiting authors
to and from the airport and she doesn't want
to do it anymore. "That's it?" I said.
"Friction over who has to pick up the big shots
from the airport? That's all you've got?"
Laughing, but really looking for conflict,
intrigue, gross incompetence, juicy misconduct,
while silently noting that no one offers to drive *me*.
And then I launched into my spiel about MFA
programs, their plenitude, the dependency they
spawn, churning out poets by the hundreds
every year. "We don't need any more poets,"
I said. "We have more than enough already."
I tossed off Philip Larkin's remark about how
he missed the days when writing poetry was slightly
disreputable and you had to hide your notebook
under the bed when somebody knocked at the door.
I trotted out my anecdote about giving a talk
at the AWP conference on finding work
outside academia and how a young woman,

a recent graduate of an MFA program,
raised her hand to express her anxiety that
without a workshop and prompts and deadlines
she wouldn't be able to write, and my first thought
was, well, in that case, YOU'RE NOT A WRITER.
Of course, I didn't say that then, but here I was
proudly proclaiming my un-empathic thought,
holding up my meanness as if it were wisdom.
And then quoting Flannery O'Connor who,
when asked if she thought universities
were stifling young writers, replied:
"They don't stifle enough of them."
At this point, my friend frowned a little,
but did that slow me down? Not at all.
I pulled out another practiced remark about
how in America anything worth doing
is worth overdoing and if having 20
MFA programs is good, 200 is even better!
And thus the glut of mediocre writers,
with the unspoken implication that all this
noise was drowning out the brilliance
of my own work. Young people shouldn't
be encouraged to write poetry, I said.
No one encouraged *me* to become a poet,
certainly not my parents, who thought it was
a bizarre waste of time and suggested I learn
a trade instead, and look how well I turned out.
The conversation went on in this vein for some time,
and you may notice that while I seem to be
proffering these harsh judgments as examples of ego
run amok, and thus disavowing them, I am also
giving voice to them and secretly hoping
you'll agree with at least some of them.

And then I announced that I had just been
accepted into a mindfulness meditation
teacher training program, and how excited I was
to be moving into a new kind of teaching,
bringing my spiritual practice and my poetry
into greater alignment, how I planned to offer
a weekly poetry and meditation class.
I could not feel the angels of irony looking
down on me as I said this, but I feel them now,
raising their angelic eyebrows, scratching
their celestial chins, wondering how anyone
so mired in judgment could possibly
teach mindfulness. Maybe you should try
practicing it first, I can almost hear them thinking.
And now I see that in describing/confessing
my obsessive, relentless self-concern,
I am really seeking affirmation for my honesty
and that in admitting this hidden motive
I am further promoting an image of myself
as a person of fearless self-awareness,
and so on and so forth down the infinite
hall of mirrors that is the ego and its sly
maneuverings. Ah, the ego, it won't enjoy
being spoken of in this way, pinned to the page,
undercut, exposed, its bag of tricks revealed.
Even now it's angling for an advantage, trying
to make a comeback, looking for a way to end
this poem that will bring praise, applause, a prize,
maybe even a ride to the airport.
Which is not going
to happen.

Introductions

Now I use
my

business
cards

to
squash

the ants
that

crawl
across

my desk
so im-

pudently
it's as

if they
don't

know
who I am.

I Decided to Weigh My Head

Was it really as heavy as it felt?
I got the scale out
from under the bathroom sink.
That's where it lives,
tilted on its side,
resting in its zeroes.
Would my head weigh more
than the *Collected Works*
of Anthony Trollope?
More than my overfed
tuxedo cat?
Would my jittery thoughts
balance out
my mournful ones?
Or would my head reveal itself
to be largely empty, like
the universe
which it contains,
as I'd often feared
and sometimes wished?
I realized I would need a mirror.
I lay down
on the bathroom tile,
pillowed the scale
under the back of my skull,
held the hand-mirror at arm's length,
and took a good look
at myself,
the absurdity of my situation,
a grown man lying
between toilet and tub

wearing the slightly
self-mocking
anticipatory expression
of a person who has decided
to weigh his head.
The number floated above me
as in a thought bubble
and I had my answer: 8.8 lbs.,
two infinities
turned right side up,
the Eightfold Path doubled,
the number of years my father lived
minus the decimal,
and about half as heavy
as I'd imagined
this thing my spine had evolved
to lift into the air and carry
above the earth
would be.

Genius Offshore

Standing in the
ocean

calm for
a long while

when three
big ones

lift me up
knock me

down and
I realize even

the waves
come in waves.

No Day at the Beach

It's no day at the beach
being me, I said.
It's no walk
in the park.
I can see that,
she said.
Trust me, I said.
It's no picnic.
Clearly, she said.
What's that
supposed
to mean? I said.
I'm just agreeing
with you, she
said. You might
have argued
a bit, I said. Tried
to convince me
otherwise.
Who knows,
maybe it *is*
a day at the beach
being me. Or
maybe it's a day
at the beach
being *with* me.
No, she said. It's not.

Birds of a Feather

My mind combines all the qualities
of screeching crow, catbird,
vulture, hummingbird,
and the lowly, greenish-gray

pigeon. Which is to say
it is a duplicitous chatterbox
that can't be satisfied, though
it feeds on death itself;

that it needles the air
with its nervousness
and pecks the ground for crumbs,
oblivious to the vast sky above.

God gave it wings but it has
turned them into shovels,
prefers tunneling to flying,
dark and self-created caves

to infinite, unasked-for freedom.
Prefers thinking to seeing,
self to other, elsewhere
to here. Prefers preferring

above all. Perched atop the tall
tree of my spine, it squawks
and chatters and sings,
judgmental, foolish and afraid,

and will not cease until it finds
something wrong with everything.

Sightlines

We'll have to shear off the tops of those trees
if they continue to block my view
of the mountain. Not only our trees
but the neighbors' as well. Find some
daredevil to fly a helicopter upside
down over the neighborhood
and give it a good haircut.
It's America, people will do anything.
And my sightline is sacrosanct.
I need to see that peak floating
like Fuji, not just know it's there.
So I can orient my immaterial
longings, my desire to transcend
earthly limitations. I can't be
expected to pray to something
half obscured by these lesser gods
etching themselves into the evening air,
performing their fantastic
collaborations with the wind, keeping
or dropping their needles or leaves,
subject as they are to time and change.
What can they teach me about how to be?

The Empty Chair

Waiting for the poetry reading
to get started, I turn around
to apologize to the man
sitting diagonally behind me
for blocking his view.
I am tall, the back of my head
has absorbed a thousand
silent curses at movies, concerts,
theatrical performances, etc.
But he says it's OK,
thanks me for my thoughtfulness.
My friend sitting next to me
offers to switch seats
so I can stretch my legs
into the aisle but I say no,
if I sat there I'd *really* block his view—
unless my head were to become
suddenly transparent,
which I wish it would do,
the solid self, the illusion
of the solid self, gone:
just eyes and ears to see
and hear with, otherwise
vacant space, clean, open, clear,
like a window a breeze
blows into, billowing
the white diaphanous curtains,
and there's an empty chair
where a man once sat
reading, thinking, thinking
of nothing, offering no
obstruction, nothing to obstruct.

Intrigue in the Trees

Horse-collared by the high heat
of mountainous afternoons,
dogged by furious
dissatisfactions,
snake-bit, buffaloed,
bird-brained. Thank you,
animals, for giving us so many
useful metaphors and forgive us
for disappearing you,
daily and eternally.
Often I wonder:
is the earth trying to get
rid of us, shake us off,
drown us, scorch us
to nothingness?
To save itself and all other
creatures slated for extinction?
The trees around here
seem friendly enough—
stoic, philosophically inclined
toward nonjudgmental
awareness and giving
in their branchings
perfect examples
of one thing becoming two
and remaining one—
but who knows
what they really feel?
Just last night I was walking
to my favorite cafe,
The Laughing Goat,

when I saw a murder of crows
circling rain-cloudy sky,
arguing, speaking strangely,
suddenly alight on
a maple tree, dozens of them
closing down their wings
like arrogant, ill-tempered
magistrates. Everybody
was looking up and
watching. Some kind of
consultation was happening there
(animals think we're crazy
for thinking they can't think),
and I said to a woman
passing on the sidewalk:
I wonder what they're
planning. She laughed and
kept right on going,
happy as a lark.

In Brooklyn

a whoosh
of wind

whipped
my hat

right off
spun it up-

ward thirty
feet in air

my black
felt fedora

no driver
would stop

or even
swerve for

on rush hour
Flatbush

Avenue—
there it was

high above
the street

flopping and
leaping

like an
erratic over-

excited kite
or like the

thoughts it sits
on top of

as if my mind
had tried

to fly away
(where

would it
go?) and

taken my hat
with it but

the wind
dropped it

at my feet
unharmed

like Dorothy
after the

tornado—
I clamped

it on my
head and

crossing the
crosswalk

counted
it a miracle.

Etiquette

Here in New
York City

smiling is
frowned

upon and
looking

up looked
down upon.

Thin Man

The slant of this
particular

sunset casts
my shadow

absurdly long
it ambles out

stretches out
twenty feet

in front of me
a stylish Eiffel

Tower shaped
figure ta-

pering toward
the top—

now I am what
I've always

wanted to be:
a Giacometti

sculpture
that could walk.

Greatness

I fell asleep at the great poet's reading last night.
It was such a pleasure to feel myself slipping
off the blurred and queenly self-importance
of her words into blissful wandering dream-state,

my chin bouncing off my chest once or twice
and not to resist the unconsciousness
she seemed almost deliberately to inspire.

At the applause I awoke refreshed.
"That was great," I said, and the man sitting
in front of me said, "Yes, it doesn't get
much better than that."

Nebraska

After watching
Nebraska

a film shot
entirely

in black
& white

in my
home state

I told my
friend as

the credits
rolled

"You know,
they shot

that in
color, that's

just what
Nebraska

looks
like" and

he said
"Really?"

and I said
"Jesus, no,

man,"
secretly

happy he
considered it.

Spellbound

When the spelling bee contestant
asks for the definition
of the word, the judge says:
"There is no definition."
And I think, how can that be?
A word by definition has a definition,
which is to say, "a statement
of the exact meaning of a word,
especially in a dictionary,"
which is itself defined as
"a book or electronic resource
that lists the words of a language
and gives their meaning,
or gives the equivalent words
in a different language."
Other words, in other words:
an infinite regression all the way
back to Stone Age silence.
But if that which cannot
be named cannot be known,
does it follow that that which
cannot be known cannot exist?
That is, is knowability a necessary
precondition for existence?
That's another question,
and who could possibly know
the answer, or spell it correctly?
Certainly not our contestant,
whose blank look roughly
corresponds to the empty space
where the definition

she's asking for should be.
But for a word to be a word
doesn't it have to mean *something*?
In my book, everything, even nothing,
means something.

Walk the Talk

Sometimes
I think

human
beings

are just
a way

for words
to walk

around
on earth

and
words

just a way
for wind

to hear
itself think.

Time-Out

I cannot save her, she will be broken, is broken,
will be broken again and again, this little girl,
five or six, in a grubby pink dress,
black hair, fat cheeks, hard blue eyes
on her father—a giant version of herself
inflated by time and half-controlled
rage. He grabs her shoulders
and shoves her down on the sidewalk,
against the brick wall of the bookstore
I'm about to enter, and stands back
waiting as she gets up, tries to run
past him—unstoppable force,
immovable object—and grabs her again,
slams her down, the exact same motions
but harder this time, both of them
like marionettes the god who rules over
ruined childhoods guides with gnarled fingers,
and my hardwired, Paleolithic radar
for violence flares inside me, turns me
toward them, makes me want to slam him
into the next universe. Horrible things
will happen today that none of us can stop,
savage human fear everywhere in full swing,
the need for comfort neverending,
need beyond all depth and measure,
everything will happen and none can stop it,
but *this* will not happen, not here, not now,
though she will be broken, and I say,
"Hey, man, you do that again, I'm calling
the cops—*what* is going on here?"
"She's having a time-out," he says,

"call the cops if you want to," and the raspy
mother smoking on the street corner says,
"She's having a time-out, that's good discipline,
daddy," and I stand there, held in this moment,
and then he starts to gentle her, sets her
softly down, she snarls her lip, sputters
up at him, five-year-old for go fuck yourself,
and I think good for you and he calls her
honey, kneels down close to talk to her,
and I can't tell if it's a show for me or if it's real,
though I can feel he feels my eyes on him,
and I'm not going anywhere, until he takes
her hand and walks her inside the bookstore,
a wavering illusion of loving father
and trusting child, and I follow them
to where all the helpless words are kept
and time itself rests inside the covers
waiting to be set free now and forever
and he lets me walk away.

Circle

The small steel circle pressed against
the back of my head could have
opened up a whole

new world—red flashing down
corridors of hospitals and churches
and earth that leads to

the deathless realm of the dead,
the door to which is everywhere
so easily opened, living

tremblingly just below the world
we live in and think will last
forever. But this is just

an apparition of everything we've
wished for and feared, the mind's
rough elaboration

of itself in the shape of a city, filled
with stray obsessive thoughts
colliding and recombining,

crowding each other out or hunting
each other down. Which thought
was he an embodiment of,

the man who stepped out of the night
like a feverish piece of the night
itself and jammed a gun

against my head? The wish to be
released from all thinking,
granted at last? The need

to enter a world other than this one,
more lasting and more real? Or
my own unacknowledged

fury unleashed, years ago, and come
full circle now to find its source
in the fear in my eyes?

Field of Vision

Our survival cost us our happiness,
always scanning for lions
stalking the open

savannahs—is that
a panther or just wind
in the tall grass moving?

The careless became
a big cat's satisfied sleep.
The rest of us are here,

five million years of fear
hardwiring our brains
to be on guard, to look

for trouble, for the one
thing wrong with this picture,
whatever the picture might be.

Now we do it out of habit,
even when there's no reason,
when we're perfectly safe,

walking out each morning
under the baobab trees, naked,
into the lion's field of vision.

Dick's Kitchen Metaphysical

When I set aside the book about knowledge
of higher worlds and how to attain it,
dog-earing the passage that explains
why the initiate must listen without
judgment to whatever is being said,
however contrary or noxious it might be,
the waitress at Dick's Kitchen asks me
if I'm still "working on everything."
And I answer "yes" because I'm not only
lingering over my turkey burger
and sweet yam "not fries" but pondering
questions of life and death and how to
access the mystical realm that shimmers
like a heat mirage at the center of all things.
But when she further inquires if my food
"is still tasting well," I feel myself plummeting
back into the lower worlds where all I do
is silently correct my fellow human beings
for the way they dress or drive or speak or think,
peppering them with sarcastic questions
or barking at them in my head like
a full-blown crazy person: *HOW COULD*
YOU VOTE FOR THAT APOPLECTIC
ORANGE-FACED RACIST IGNORAMUS?
or *OH FOR THE LOVE OF CHRIST YES YOU*
CAN TURN RIGHT ON RED THAT'S BEEN
A RULE FOR ABOUT FORTY YEARS
I GUESS THEY FORGOT TO TELL YOU!
But then I remember the section on
patience, forbearance, and non-anger
(which I had been tempted to skip) that says:

"Every symptom of impatience produces
a paralyzing effect on the higher faculties."
And suddenly I see them, my higher faculties,
frozen like statues, in attitudes of agony
and strife, like Rodin's prisoners
or Michelangelo's slaves: wisdom languishing
in chains, compassion with downcast eyes,
kindness struggling to rise
from the stone.

Opening

I only thought
to light a

candle but
nicked

a hole in this
world and

the unseen
burning

world came
right through.

Winter Sky, with Crows

The crows zigzag in freezing wind,
tilt their wings and glide,
lofted upward on the updrafts
and then the downward
swoop and dive,
pushed by gusts or buffeted
against them, held still
for a moment before turning
and slipping back into the current—
and then the hard work of finding
direction, flapping into it,
driving forward at all costs.

Now the sky is clear of them,
the leafless branches of the trees
stand forth, stark black,
backlit by sunrise, the space
between them empty, like
a mind suddenly free
of thought.

Something and Nothing

There's something to be said
for having nothing to say,

though I don't know what
that is, or isn't, just as

there's something to be
known about not-knowing,

which I would tell you
if I could. There must be

something to be gained
by losing, a seed of victory

buried in every failure,
else I would not be here.

Clearly, there's something
to be desired about being

beyond desire, as the sages
never tire of telling us,

and nothing more fulfilling
than emptying yourself out—

no ground beneath your feet,
nothing to hold onto, no handrail,

no belief, only this bright self-
sustaining air, and a falling

that feels like floating.

Second Sight

When I kiss you
you smudge

my glasses
so I can

hardly see
straight

and the
hard world

softens
and blurs—

words for
once

release us
and in this

darkness
the way

ahead
comes clear.

Disputed Theory

Now it's the
moon causes

volcanic
eruptions?

Makes that
burning under-

ground tide
leap from

earth's core
into the air?

Everything
in me says yes.

Here: An Epithalamion

Before I met you my life was, as you know,
no day at the beach. For every victory,
ten defeats; for every joyful moment,
a melancholy week; for every shapely
poem, a thick volume of silence.
I was always pining for some
golden age, thinking everything
was better back then, even
my nostalgia was better, more
piercing, more true. Wherever I was
I wanted to be somewhere else,
but when I got there I wanted to be
back where I started. Now I know
that what I wanted was to be here,
with you, though I had only a sliver of faith
I would ever find you, just a feather
from the bird of Hope. I was a glass
half broken kind of person. Ken Pallack
gave me a racehorse nickname,
Stagedoor Johnny, which I quickly
changed to *Trapdoor Johnny* and
dropped right through it.
I thought I was who I thought I was.
And when I tried to embrace my
imperfections, even my arms
fell short. And all the false starts,
wrong turns, convoluted detours,
and treacherous conditions! It seems
I had to fail at love every possible way
to make the way possible for you.
But now you're here and here is where

I want to be. Frank O'Hara said
"It is easy to be beautiful. It is
difficult to appear so." But not for you,
you're beautiful all the way through,
no disharmony between essence
and appearance, and I love you
from the surface of your skin to
the depths of your soul, and I would
gladly embrace your imperfections
if you had any, and Joseph Goldstein
says that anything can happen anytime
and that's true, but only *this* could be
happening right now, only this moment,
which is the fruit of the tree of every moment
that came before it, the secret momentum
that brought me to you and you to me
and all of us here to this garden—
only *this* moment, which as I write it
I can only imagine but as I say it
is really happening, a miracle,
right here, right now, lifted up
from time's unrelenting flow
and held within the loving sphere
of all our friends and family:
here, now, just this, forever.

Over the Moon

for Alice

Five a.m.—the soft percussion of the rain
on the slanted rooftop of my study.
I study it: a single drop dropping again
and again at one second intervals,
like the ticking of a watery clock
above my head. Off to my right,
it comes down in loose clusters,
an absentminded thrumming of fingers
on a tabletop, random, irregular,
or falling in a pattern I can't perceive.
It's too dark to see the rain as it falls,
only the reflection of my room
projected onto the empty space beyond
my *window*—an old Norse word
made from two other words: *wind* and *eye*.
My bookcases float blurrily
in the air above the alley,
I tap the keyboard and words appear,
and now the rain appears to be hesitating,
or reconsidering, though it will likely
fall all day long on the bamboo trees
I cannot see, the glory-bower, the lilacs
and azaleas readying themselves,
summoning their flowers from the depths
of nonexistence, three kinds of Japanese
maples and the improbable ferns,
huge and flamelike, heart-shaped,
that edge the yard. Last night we stopped
and stepped backward when we crossed

a sidewalk puddle where the moon
had fallen between a reflection
of rootlike branches and swiftly
passing clouds to hover underneath us.
As above, so below, the old alchemists said,
everything mirroring everything else,
falling and rising and falling.
We lingered looking down, then
stepped over the moon and came home.

ACKNOWLEDGMENTS

Thanks to the editors of the following journals for publishing some of the poems collected here, sometimes in different forms.

American Journal of Poetry: "Blathery Performance"

Barrow Street: "Tough Town"

Cloudbank: "Greatness"

The Cortland Review: "Loss and Gain"

December: "Nebraska"

The Gettysburg Review: "Swifts"

Hotel Amerika: "Wishful Thinking," "Wisteria"

The Manhattan Review: "Fedora," "Sightlines," "Field of Vision," "Birds of a Feather," "Falling Hours," "Dick's Kitchen Metaphysical," "Thin Man," "In Brooklyn," "Something and Nothing"

New Ohio Review: "Back Then," "Looking on the Bright Side"

New South: "The Vow," "The Dismal Kingdom"

Plume: "Over the Moon," "Signs and Wonderings," "I Decided to Weigh My Head"

Poetry: "Circle"

Poetry Northwest: "Sleeping in the Wind," "Walk the Talk," "Dharma Talk"

Prairie Schooner: "November"

Rattle: "Time-Out," "Etiquette"

The Sun: "No Day at the Beach," "Cold Spell," "Intrigue in the Trees," "The Empty Chair"

This Land: "Introductions"

"Intrigue in the Trees" was included in *The Best American Poetry 2017*, edited by Natasha Tretheway, series editor David Lehman.

I'm deeply grateful to Andrea Hollander, Paulann Petersen, Fred Muratori, Justin Rigamonti, and Alice Boyd for helping to make *No Day at the Beach* a better book. My thanks to Ron Wallace and everyone at the University of Wisconsin Press for bringing it into the world. Thanks also to Oregon Literary Arts for support in the form of a fellowship.

Wisconsin Poetry Series

Edited by Ronald Wallace and Sean Bishop

(B) = WINNER OF THE BRITTINGHAM PRIZE IN POETRY
(FP) = WINNER OF THE FELIX POLLAK PRIZE IN POETRY
(4L) = WINNER OF THE FOUR LAKES PRIZE IN POETRY

JOHN BREHM is the author of *Sea of Faith* and *Help Is on the Way*, both from the University of Wisconsin Press. He is the editor of *The Poetry of Impermanence, Mindfulness, and Joy* and the associate editor of *The Oxford Book of American Poetry*. His poems have appeared in *Poetry*, *New Ohio Review*, *The Sun*, *Poetry Northwest*, *The Gettysburg Review*, *Plume*, *The Southern Review*, *Best American Poetry*, *The Writer's Almanac*, and many other journals and anthologies. He lives in Portland, Oregon.

JOHNBREHMPOET.COM